For the grown-ups

This book is full of hands-on activities that will tap straight into your child's natural scientific curiosity and engineering creativity. Each activity is designed to let your child play and learn with all their senses. Together, you can grow their love of science, their engineering ingenuity, and their understanding of the world.

Here are a few tips to help you along the way:

Your child should be supervised at all times when conducting these experiments, but try to give them time and space to lead the direction of play. The questions in this book are suggestions. Let your child ask their own questions, and try out their own ideas.

•

Involve your child in the preparation of each activity. Let them follow the instructions but also let them try out their own ideas and explore the investigations in ways that they find interesting. You never know what they might discover!

•

Adult Alert stars show where your child will need extra grown-up help.

•

Protect the area where your child will be playing and encourage them to wear old clothes. Being prepared lets your child enjoy themselves to their fullest. Making a mess is part of the fun and learning!

Adult ALERT

DK | Penguin Random House

Series Editor Hêlène Hilton
Senior Designer and Illustrator Rachael Parfitt Hunt
Editor Sally Beets
US Senior Editor Shannon Beatty
US Editor Mindy Fichter
Editorial Assistance Violet Peto
Additional Design and Illustration Eleanor Bates, Charlotte Bull, Kitty Glavin, Charlotte Milner
Educational Consultant Penny Coltman
Photographer Lol Johnson
Additional Photography Dave King
Jacket Designers Charlotte Milner, Eleanor Bates
Jacket Coordinator Francesca Young
Producer, Pre-Production Dragana Puvacic
Senior Producer Amy Knight
Managing Editor Penny Smith
Managing Art Editor Mabel Chan
Publisher Mary Ling
Creative Director Helen Senior

A catalog record for this book
is available from the Library of Congress.
ISBN: 978-1-4654-6857-4

DK books are available at special discounts when purchased in bulk for sales promotions, premiums, fund-raising, or educational use. For details, contact: DK Publishing Special Markets, 345 Hudson Street, New York, New York 10014 SpecialSales@dk.com

Printed and bound in China

The publisher would like to thank the following for their kind permission to reproduce their photographs:
(Key: a-above; b-below/bottom; c-center; f-far; l-left; r-right; t-top)
8-9 Getty Images: Navaswan / The Image Bank (t/sky). **13 Getty Images:** Navaswan / The Image Bank (sky). **14-15 Getty Images:** Navaswan / The Image Bank (sky). **17 Dreamstime.com:** Vladvitek (tr). **28 123RF.com:** Peter Jeffreys / petejeff (br). All other images © Dorling Kindersley.
For further information see: www.dkimages.com

And a **big thank you** to all the little engineers who acted as models – Isaac Abban, Hannah Bollito, India Noone, Anais Rahman, Rafferty Smale, and Tobi Saggar. **Extra thanks** also to Alex Hilton for his invaluable engineering expertise and advice.

First American Edition, 2018
Published in the United States by DK Publishing
345 Hudson Street, New York, New York 10014

Copyright © 2018 Dorling Kindersley Limited
A Penguin Random House Company
18 19 20 21 22 10 9 8 7 6 5 4 3 2 1
001–307629–August/2018

A WORLD OF IDEAS:
SEE ALL THERE IS TO KNOW

www.dk.com

Contents

Little minds have big ideas!

You don't need **safety boots, a yellow hard hat,** and **fancy tools** to be an awesome engineer. You already have everything you need: **your brain** and **your amazing senses**!

Curious questions

By asking yourself engineering questions, you create better things. Here are some questions to ask yourself as you play.

- Why am I creating this?

- How can I try making it a different way?

- What can I hear, smell, see, taste, and feel?

- How can I make this even better?

Your engineering senses

Brain
Your brain is not one of your senses, but it gathers information from them all and tries to understand it.

Hearing
There are so many noises to listen to! What can you hear?

Sight
Awesome engineers use their eyes to see how things work.

Smell
Use your nose to find smelly clues!

Taste
Your tongue is great at tasting different flavors.

Let's see what we can do!

Touch
Your skin tells you how things feel. Be careful with objects that might be hot, cold, sharp, or that might hurt.

Painting gravity

Gravity is the thing that **pulls** your feet back to the **ground** when you **jump**. Make this awesome **paint pendulum** to prove that **gravity** really is there.

You might want to do this outside since it can get messy!

You will need:

Adult ALERT!

paint mixed with a little water

sticky tack

scissors

plastic bottle with the bottom cut off

Set your pendulum up like this

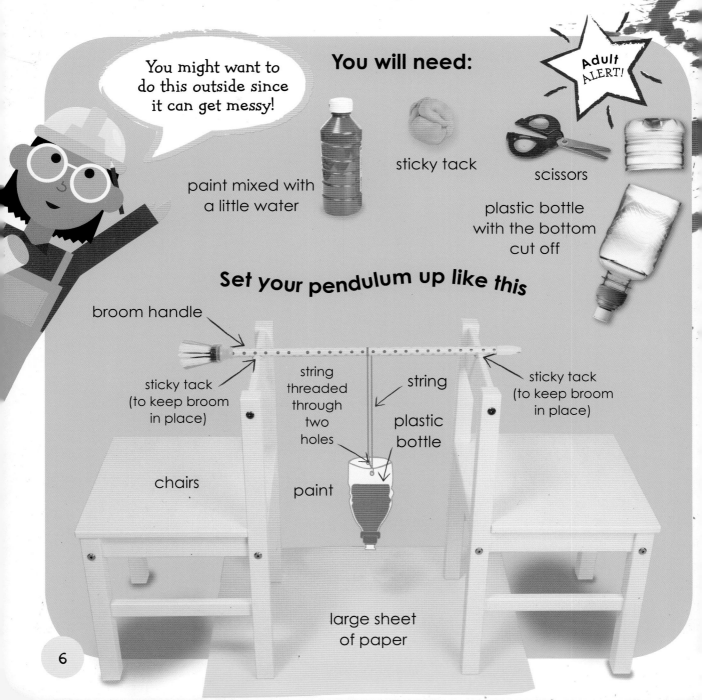

broom handle

sticky tack (to keep broom in place)

string threaded through two holes

string

sticky tack (to keep broom in place)

plastic bottle

chairs

paint

large sheet of paper

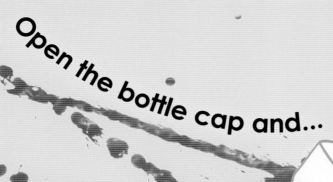

Open the bottle cap and...

Swish!

Try changing the **color of paint** in the bottle to make really interesting **patterns**.

swing your pendulum!

What's a pendulum?

A pendulum is a **heavy** thing at the end of a string. If you **push** it, it **swings** away. It then **swings back**, because **gravity pulls** it. Your push and gravity's pull make it **swing**.

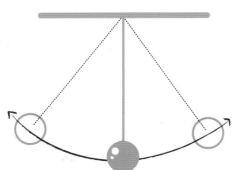

EXPLORE
engineering

 How will you display your beautiful design?

 Can you feel gravity pulling you down? Why or why not?

What happens if you make your string shorter?

Parachute launch

Gravity pulls everything back to **Earth**, and parachutes are a great way to get **safely** back to the ground. Which of these parachutes works the **best**?

You will need:

Use little toy people or make me from pipe cleaners.

make each square the same size

three squares of different materials (we are using shopping bag plastic, fabric, and a napkin)

pipe cleaner people or little toys

scissors

string

1 Snip a **small hole** in each corner of your squares of material and **tie a piece of string** to each hole.

2 Tie the other ends of the **string** to your little people. Then **drop** them from a height.

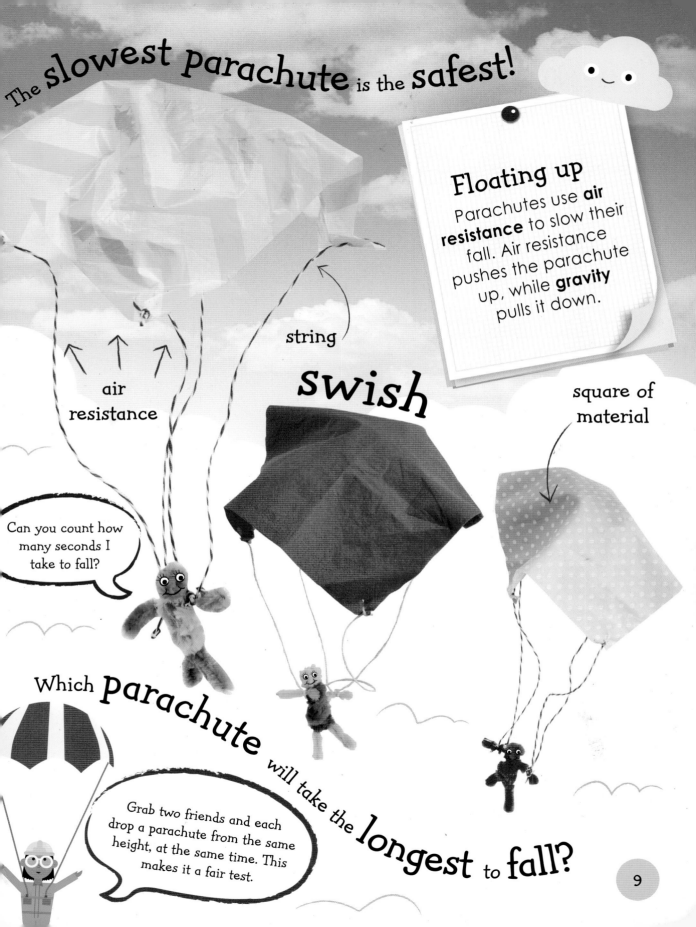

The **slowest parachute** is the **safest!**

Floating up

Parachutes use **air resistance** to slow their fall. Air resistance pushes the parachute up, while **gravity** pulls it down.

string

swish

air resistance

square of material

Can you count how many seconds I take to fall?

Which **parachute** will take the **longest** to **fall?**

Grab two friends and each drop a parachute from the same height, at the same time. This makes it a fair test.

9

Floating in the air

You may not always be able to **feel** the **air** around you, but it can be very strong. Make this **toy** that **uses air** from your **lungs** to push a ball up!

You will need:

pencil

glue and brush

scissors

straw

plate or something circular

adhesive tape

pom-poms
(you could also use aluminum foil balls or a ping-pong ball)

construction paper

Adult ALERT!

1

Draw **around a plate** on construction paper and cut out the **circle**.

2

Fold the paper in half, and then fold it in half again.

3

Cut away one segment.

Make the remaining segments into a cone shape, and glue together.

Snip a tiny hole in the cone.

4

Poke the straw **through the hole** and tape in place. Put the ball in the cone and **blow!**

Blowing fast into the straw makes a kind of mini wind called air resistance.

You can decorate your cone to look like a monster!

EXPLORE engineering

How high can you make your ball float?

Can you hear the air flowing through your straw?

Why does the ball fall back down after floating up?

Blow as hard as you can!

straw

hole

Best paper plane

There are a lot of ways to make a **paper plane**, but this is our favorite. Welcome aboard!

You will need:

paper rectangles

1
Fold the paper **in half** lengthwise to get a fold line down the **middle**. Open it up again.

2
Fold down the **top corners** to meet the middle line.

3

Adult
ALERT!

Fold down the **top corners** again to meet the middle line as shown.

4

Fold the plane **in half** along the middle line.

5

On each side of the plane, **fold down** the wings as shown.

EXPLORE
engineering

Would paper be a good material to build a real plane? Why or why not?

Why do you think your plane falls to the ground?

Can you hear your plane flying through the air? Can you hear real planes outside?

Making your plane **heavier** could actually make it **go farther!** Glue **buttons** to it and see what happens.

This plane has the same number of buttons on each wing. Why do you think this is important?

How do planes take off?

When a plane moves **forward** quickly, air rushes over the wings creating a force called **lift**. This is stronger than the **pull** of **gravity**, so the plane can take off.

Test your paper plane by throwing it and measuring how far it travels.

lift

gravity

Make a **rescue** raft

Your toys are **stranded** on a desert island! Can you rescue them by making the best **floating raft**?

You will need:

- paint
- sticky tack
- fabric
- craft sticks or twigs
- glue and brush
- scissors

1

Glue three craft sticks together to make a **frame**. Cover the frame in glue then lay more sticks **across** it.

Stick down... *...in a* **row.**

2

Paint your raft.

Wind power

A real sailboat catches the wind in its sail to move forward.

sail

Decorate your boat with a sail by gluing **fabric** to a craft stick. Stick it to the raft with tack.

3

Make a **cardboard** raft from an egg carton. The egg holes can be **seats** for your toys.

Land, ahoy! You can make toy sailors like us out of corks.

Build a boat
that goes

Lots of real boats have **propellers** that **spin** in the water to **move** them **forward**. Make your own boat that really moves!

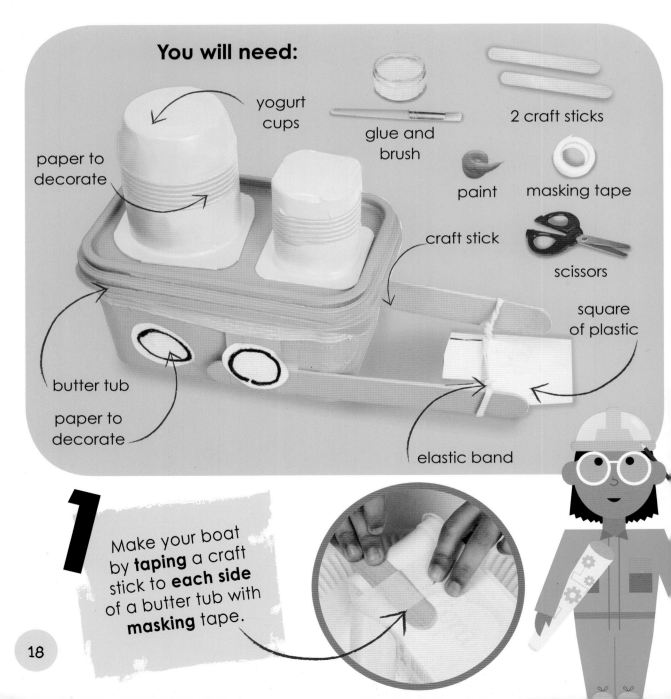

You will need:

- yogurt cups
- glue and brush
- paint
- 2 craft sticks
- masking tape
- paper to decorate
- craft stick
- scissors
- square of plastic
- butter tub
- paper to decorate
- elastic band

1 Make your boat by **taping** a craft stick to **each side** of a butter tub with **masking** tape.

2

Paint and decorate your boat. You can also **glue** yogurt cups to the lid for **funnels**.

Decorate your...

brilliant boat!

3

Make a propeller

Stretch the **elastic band** around both sticks. Cut out a **square of plastic** from the lid of another butter tub and snip **two notches** into it to make your propeller. Slide it onto the elastic band.

Wind the propeller around and around.

Elastic power

By **winding** the **elastic band** on your propeller, you stretch it and give it **energy**. Then when you let it go, it releases all that energy, spins the propeller, and makes your boat **go**.

Put your boats to the test

All aboard! It's time to find out which **raft or boat is best** for rescuing your toys from the desert island.

Test the **boats** to see if they *float!*

Which **material** is best for making a boat that **floats**? A **plastic** butter tub, a **cardboard** egg carton or **wooden** craft sticks? Put them in water to find out!

The butter tub boat is a box **filled with air**. This makes it **light for its size** and extra good at **floating**.

splash

splish

How do boats float?

A special force called buoyancy pushes things up in water so that they float.

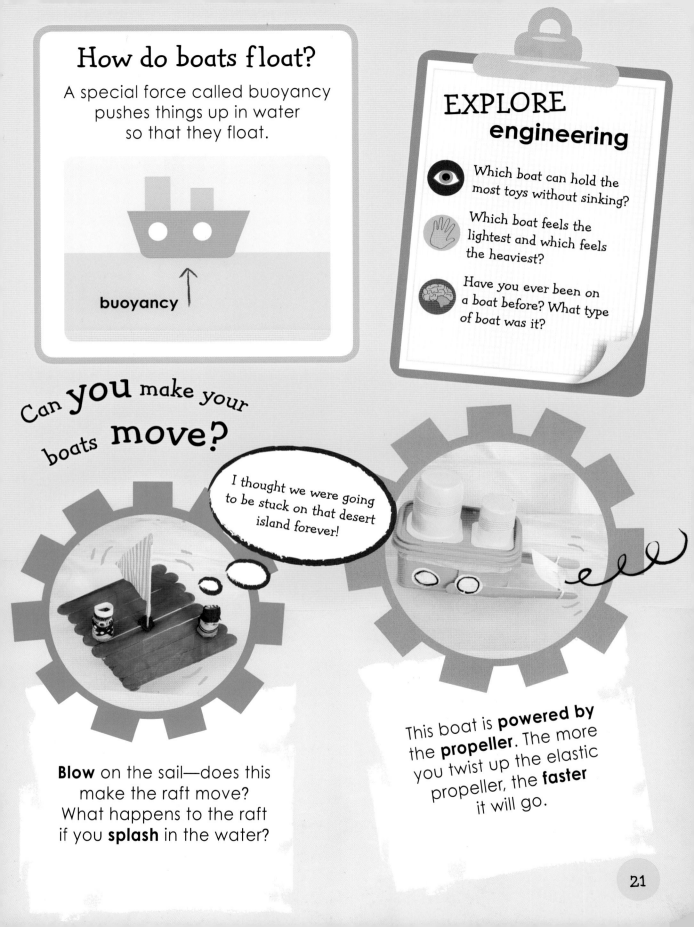

buoyancy

EXPLORE engineering

Which boat can hold the most toys without sinking?

Which boat feels the lightest and which feels the heaviest?

Have you ever been on a boat before? What type of boat was it?

Can **you** make your boats **move?**

I thought we were going to be stuck on that desert island forever!

Blow on the sail—does this make the raft move? What happens to the raft if you **splash** in the water?

This boat is **powered by** the **propeller**. The more you twist up the elastic propeller, the **faster** it will go.

21

Sunny, funny stove

Our **sun** is a huge ball of **burning gas** that gives off a lot of **heat**. It gives our planet **light** and **warmth**. You can use the heat from the sun to make some **tasty treats**.

aluminum foil

You will need:

ruler

pencil

adhesive tape

plastic wrap

glue and brush

scissors

black paper

pizza box

marshmallows and cookies

pencil

ruler

1

Draw three lines of a **square** onto the box lid and carefully cut these to **make a flap**.

Adult ALERT!

2

Glue foil to the **inside of the flap**. Make sure the shiniest side is facing out.

Stick it down.

foil

nesive
ape

plastic wrap

3

Open the box lid and **tape plastic wrap** to the inside of the square you've cut.

4

Put black paper inside the box. Place your **marshmallows** and **cookies** on top of the paper.

Dark or shiny?

Dark colored things **absorb heat**. That means they get hot quickly. **Shiny things** do the opposite—they push light and heat away from them. **Heat and light** from the sun will **bounce** off the shiny foil toward your food. The dark paper will absorb the heat. Together they **warm up** your food.

5

Prop the lid open...

ruler

with a ruler or a stick.

I'm feeling a litle hot in here!

6

Carefully **turn** your stove so that the **sun** is **shining** straight into it.

Wait for your tasty treats to be ready.

This might take a little while depending on how hot and sunny it is.

24

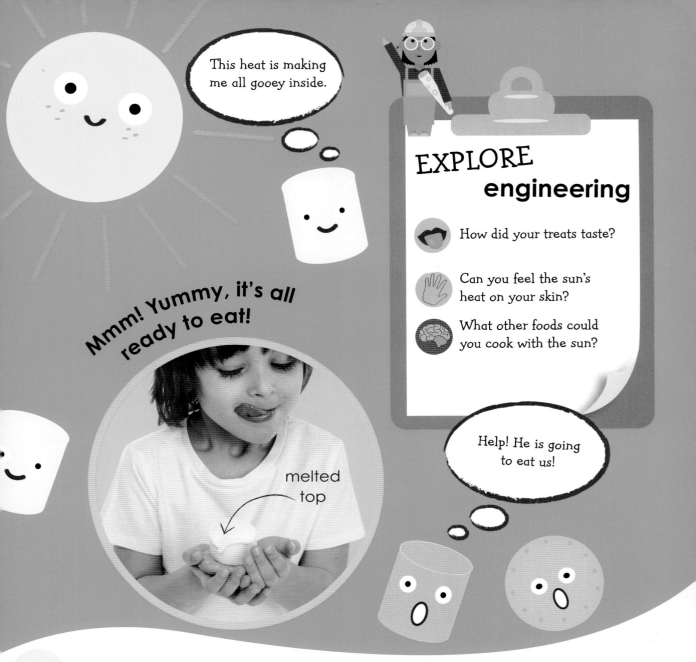

This heat is making me all gooey inside.

EXPLORE
engineering

How did your treats taste?

Can you feel the sun's heat on your skin?

What other foods could you cook with the sun?

Mmm! Yummy, it's all ready to eat!

melted top

Help! He is going to eat us!

Green energy

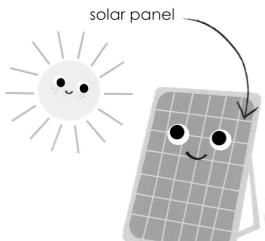

solar panel

The light we get from **the sun** is a **renewable energy**, or green energy. That means it doesn't harm the planet and it will not get used up. **Solar panels** use the **sun's energy** to make **electricity.** Some people put solar panels on their roofs to **power** their homes.

25

Magical woodland den

Whether you are creating this **little home** for a **fairy** or a **gnome**, make it **super strong** and safe with the **magic** of **engineering**.

You will need:

sticks

ribbons

leaves and twigs

string

toys
(optional)

paintbrush

paint

1

Choose **two sticks** that are the same length and **tie them together** with a piece of string.

Tie a knot.

two sticks

2

Add a **third stick** and cross it over at the top. Tie it in place to make a **tripod**.

Carefully balance the sticks in place.

This den is called a tepee.

3

Tie a fourth stick in place and **stand** the tepee up.

triangle shape

Triangles

Triangles are shapes with **three straight sides**. These strong shapes are used a lot in **engineering**. How many triangles can you **spot** in your den so far?

Wrap pretty ribbon around some of the twigs.

Decorate your den.

Paint a stick.

4

leaves

Add **leaves, mud,** and **decorated sticks** to your tepee to make **walls** and to **stop** the **rain** from coming in.

Peek inside this giant...

Head to the woods with a friend (and an adult) to make a human-sized den!

woodland den!

Which magical creatures live in your den?

Put down leaves to make a comfy floor for us!

Weatherproof

Mud is a great **building material** because it's hard and strong when it dries. Build the den in a **sheltered spot** to protect it from the rain and wind.

Wow!

29

Insect homes

Make your **backyard** or **windowsill** the perfect place for **bugs to hang out** and be **happy**! Who knows what might **come to visit?**

Bee house

Bees love to have **little holes to sleep in**. Make this easy bee house by **filling a plant pot** full of sticks. Bamboo sticks are best, but any sticks will work.

plant pot

bamboo sticks

Adult ALERT!

Tie string around your pot.

Hang your special bug home **from a tree** ready for the bees.

How many insects can you find?

rolled up cardboard

straw

lavender

Adult ALERT!

seed heads

sticks and leaves

moss

Bees are super **important**

Bees are **pollinators**. That means that when they fly from **flower to flower** they help make more plants grow! Place your bug hotel **close to flowers** to help them.

What time is check in?

Insect hotel

Make an insect hotel with a lot of rooms! Fill plant pots with **different natural materials** to attract all kinds of creepy-crawlies. Carefully **stack the pots** up like a multistory hotel.

Building bridges

Bridges are great to get **over obstacles**. But building a **long** and **strong** bridge can be tricky! Can you play with **shapes** to engineer the **strongest paper bridge**?

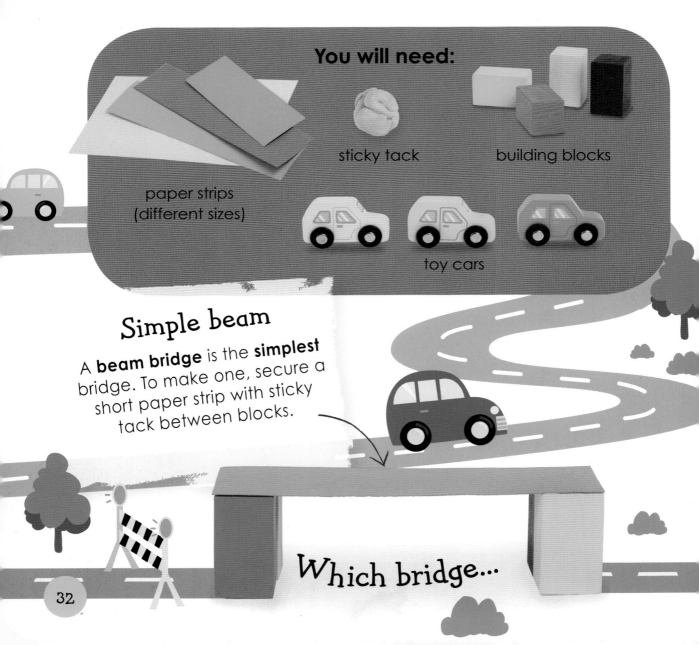

You will need:

sticky tack

building blocks

paper strips (different sizes)

toy cars

Simple beam

A **beam bridge** is the **simplest** bridge. To make one, secure a short paper strip with sticky tack between blocks.

Which bridge...

Long beam

Sometimes you need a long bridge to go farther. Can you make a **longer beam bridge**?

Curvy arch

To make an **arch bridge**, start with a beam bridge and carefully place a **curved** strip of paper underneath.

Zigzag triangles

Fold a strip of paper to make a **zigzag shape**. Put it under a beam to make a **truss bridge**.

is strongest?

Use toy cars to test the strength...

of your bridges ↓

Gravity is a force that pulls objects down. Bridges need to be strong to hold against gravity.

Long beam bridge
Gravity is pulling this car down and bending the bridge

Bridge testing
The **strength** of a bridge depends on how it spreads out **weight**. Look at the arrows to see how weight is **spread** out in each bridge.

How many cars can your bridges hold without bending?

Arch bridge
The weight of the cars is spread through the arch.

> Short beam bridges work fine if they don't carry anything too heavy.

EXPLORE engineering

👁 Can you see the bridges bend under the cars' weight?

✋ Can you feel the weight of the cars in your hand?

🧠 What materials do you think real bridges are made from?

Truss bridge
Weight is spread out along the triangle zigzags.

Sweet pyramid

A pyramid is a **pointy** shape with **triangular sides**. The Ancient Egyptians built stone **pyramids** for their **kings** and **queens**. You can make a little one with **sugar cube bricks**.

You will need:

Spoon some powdered sugar into a bowl and add water until you get a thick, sticky paste.

warm water

powdered sugar

lots of sugar cubes

1

Build a **square base** with sugar cubes. Make sure each side has the same number of cubes.

spoon

Builders use mortar to stick bricks together. Our mortar is sugar! We don't know if the Egyptians used mortar to build the pyramids.

2 Build up your pyramid by adding **layers** of smaller squares with some **sticky mortar** between each layer.

last cube

EXPLORE engineering

How does your pyramid taste?

How do you think the Egyptians made their pyramids?

Try prodding or shaking your pyramid when the powdered sugar has set. How stable is it?

The **Ancient Egyptians** built pyramids thousands of years ago, with no machines to help. Lots of them are still there. Most pyramids have **smooth sides**, but the very first ones had **steps**, just like yours.

Pyramid of Djoser

Sprinkle brown sugar.

Lick your pyramid to find out how it tastes but don't eat it!

37

Moving pictures

Way before we had movie theaters, TVs, and tablets, people used little **pictures** to make stories that **moved**. What picture will you bring to life?

You will need:

card stock

scissors

double-sided adhesive tape

pencil

1 Cut out two **card stock circles**. Draw a **flower** on one side and a **butterfly** on the other side.

Stick!

2

Using double-sided adhesive tape, **stick** the drawings back to back with the **pencil between** them.

3

Roll the pencil **quickly** between your hands. What do you **see**?

If you spin the pencil fast enough, your eyes get tricked into seeing the two pictures merge together as one.

Spin! Spin! Spin!

Cartoons

Some **cartoons** you see on TV are really made up of a lot of **still drawings**. Each drawing is slightly different so when they're **put together** it looks like the characters are moving.

Rainbow lights

This really cool toy is a **kaleidoscope.** Make your own kaleidoscope to see how **light** bounces off **shiny** things.

You will need:

Adult ALERT!

aluminum foil

plastic wrap

card stock rectangles

potato chip cannister with a clear lid

small colorful things, like glitter beads, and sequins

glue and brush

adhesive tape

1

Glue the not-so-shiny side of the **aluminum foil** onto the card stock.

Fold the card stock into three (lengthwise) as shown. **Tape the edges** together, then **slide** the **folded card stock** into the tube.

Tape here.

You can decorate your tube with colorful paper if you want to.

Shiny things

Things that are shiny **reflect light**. Light bounces off them and this makes it look like there are two of the same thing—the real thing and its **reflection**. In your kaleidoscope, there are **three shiny mirrors**, so it looks like there are lots of the same objects.

The word kaleidoscope means "look at all the beautiful shapes" in Ancient Greek.

3

Place a lot of **small, pretty things** inside the lid. You can **glue** some pieces and leave others loose.

4

Cover inside of the lid with plastic wrap and put the lid back on the **tube** with the plastic wrap **stretched tightly**.

5

Cut off the excess plastic wrap from around the **edges**.

Adult ALERT!

6 Carefully use scissors to poke an **eye hole** into the other end of the tube.

EXPLORE
engineering

Someone has to eat the chips before you can use the tube! How do they taste?

What happens when you spin your kaleidoscope around?

What other reflective things can you find?

Look toward the window and spin the tube to see all the pretty shapes and colors!

Rocket engineering

Make your very own, super simple, tiny **rockets**.
What **planet** are you heading to, engineer?

You will need:

paper

markers

adhesive tape

straws

2 Cut a strip of paper and **tape** the long sides together to make a tube. Your straw should **slide** through this.

1 **Draw** a small rocket with your markers and **cut it out**. Don't make it too big or it will struggle to lift off.

Make a lot of rockets so you and your friends can have a rocket race!

3

Tape one side of tube **shut**, then tape this to the **rocket.** Leave an **opening** to slip the tube on and off the straw.

4

Place the rocket on the straw. Time for **liftoff!**

The air you blow into your launching pouch makes the rocket shoot forward.

3... 2... 1...

BLOW!

Rocket science

Real rockets burn a lot of **fuel** to launch. As it burns, the fuel makes gas. This **bursts out** of the rocket and it's so strong that the rocket **shoots away.** It is the same as your rocket, only much bigger!

45

Look, you're an engineer

Awesome **engineers** (like you) use their **brains**, their **creativity**, and all their **senses** to **invent** amazing things that make the **world** a little **happier**.

How cool is this?

Engineers use their **brains** to make **really clever**, exciting things that they can **play** with. It's all about having **fun** and being **creative**.

How useful is this?

Making a cool thing is **even better** when it's **useful** and it **helps people**. If you think of something that needs **fixing** or **inventing**, get engineering!

Can I make it work?

Once you've decided what you're going to make, work out **how** to make it. Think about what **designs** and **materials** will work best and **try them out**.

Don't give up!

When you create something **new**, it won't always work the first time... or the second time... or the third time. It might take **a while**! But you can **learn** each time and **make it better**.

There are a lot of different engineers! From building rockets, to houses, to computers, each engineer does something they love.

Good Job!

....

(Write your name here.)

is an engineer!

Index